Simple

Verse

Edited by A. B. Caudsey

Barry Seymour

euPublishing.eu

This edition first published in England 2015 by euPublishing.eu

First printed in 2015

British Library Cataloguing in Publication Data.

A catalogue record for this book is available from the British Library.

ISBN 978 0 9930619 2 9

Printed and bound in England

Selected and edited by A. B. Caudsey

"Now I will not parade and shout this out loud

In order not to further offend the maddening crowd

So I write it down with pen and paper,

And it makes me feel better to vent some anger"

from *The Politicians*

Dedicated to my Mother

Judy Seymour

Contents

Visceral

I shall just start and begin
You crawl through every inch of my vulnerable skin.
You break into my mind
And it's you in there I can always find.

You flow within the stream of my blood
Filling my heart with such love
Like a broken dam causing a flood
And my heart a beating thud, thud, thud.

You consume my senses until I'm senseless
And your passionate kisses leave me breathless.
I'm delirious and contented, in a hapless mess
My mind is spinning in a loving distress.

Head, shoulders, knees and toes
I can even feel you in my bones.
The moment you are missing it's so hard hitting
But being with you is just so befitting.

Eyes

Behind your piercing bright eyes

There lies your mysterious historic disguise

And the tracks from fallen tears

Show your broken heart and its demise.

Two bright windows that show your soul

They look at me and each time I see,

I see something new,

Something honest, something true from the depths of you.

Bright so bright like a reflective kaleidoscope so deep

They continue to haunt me in a nightly surrealist sleep.

But it's you and your bright eyes that I want to keep

No matter how much they haunt me in my sleep.

I study and marvel at those eyes with devotion

But I risk drowning in their raw emotion.

Now my soul is at stake

And looking too long could be my fatal mistake.

<u>You Are</u>

You are to me

The wind in my sails

You are to me

The one that never fails

Never fails to fill my heart and you complete my life

No matter what the trouble, no matter what the strife.

You are to me

The freshest air

You are to me

So beautiful, so fair

I never want to be apart

To be apart from you and your loving heart.

You are to me

My right and my left

You are to me

My north and south

And I'm in heaven

When I kiss your voluptuous mouth.

You are to me

So magical and fantastical

Bewitching and transfixing.

You are to me

No other words, you are my everything

You are my hope and my never ending.

Romance

It's getting late in this tranquil,

Starlit, crescent moon, constellation night,

And your aura, your deep blue eyes

Shine like meteors so very bright.

Your body is a fertile, colourful, blooming garden

With a pink, soft, fragrant rose in the middle

And I slowly, gently approach your gates

To play you sweet music with my loving fiddle.

Now inside and with the champagne flowing

Close to the fire the whole room is glowing

Fireworks start to explode and we are both filled with burning desire

And it's the passionate look in your eye which I most admire.

<u>Shining</u>

She's a shining light
Burning a Fahrenheit bright
Flaming to warm this cold winter night
She shines with all her might.

She lights the way
She could light the deepest darkest alleyway
She could light it up like a firework display
And take that freeze away.

Smouldering white hot
A shadow she is not
She's a golden girl
And a shining star that will take you far.

She Skips

She skips, splishing and splashing
Along a Cornish moonlit night beach
But she cannot swim so I stay in reach
And with joy she lets out a scream and a screech.

She performs a dance
She has me locked in a trance
Like a child so free
She kicks against the waves of the sea.

I watch in awe sitting on this secluded shore
And have never seen such beauty before.
I could sit here forever
And watch her forever more.

One Of A Kind

She's an illuminated pretty thing, one of a kind
Beauty she does bring to my eyes and mind
Bright blonde shining on my bed scantily clad
And I think to myself this day is not so bad.

Her eyelashes a batter and I cannot help but to flatter
But oh my goodness can she natter
All the same she's a blonde lioness
And her body is a glorious fortress.

Rouge are her lips
Golden are her legs, breasts and cheeks
Pretty in pink and not at all meek
Tonight is the night and it's me she will seek.

Why Do I?

Why do I have to intensely miss you so?

This morning without you gives me pangs

And it's dragging out so slow

And all I'm left with is the presence of your afterglow.

Why do I have to need you so?

Like being thirsty for water

Or hungry for food.

When you are not here this feeling is a haunting blue mood.

Why do I have to long for you so?

You have only been gone an hour so far

And my heart feels like it's trapped in a jar.

It's now feeling like a month or so and this day is going in slow mo.

I miss all of you, your face, your hair, your talk,

Your smile, your arms and legs and just the way you walk your walk,

Your nose, your lips, your bottom, your breasts,

And I'm just here feeling ever so restless.

<u>By Your Side</u>

To be by your side

There is no need to run

There is no need to hide.

Just to be with you

And enjoy this ride

Together with every step and every stride

And within you I do confide

Without you I would surely begin to subside.

With you things are divine,

Every day you're my Valentine

And I'm truly blessed

To think that you are mine.

To Be With You

To be alone with you
Is where I like to be the most
You satisfy and see me through
And when I'm with you I don't feel at all blue.

When you're here, when you are near
There is no fear to be feared
No tears to be cried
No one to tell me made up stories or destructive lies.

I can for a time forget all the rest
And I think you are undisputedly the best
And to be with you in your company
Is to be truly blessed.

You light up our four walls
Erase all the pitfalls
You have the charm and presence of a waterfall
You are my beginning and end of it all.

An American Dream

I had an American dream

Or rather I dreamed of America

To get myself out of here

Out of this Irish land of poverty and fear.

I had no shoes, I had nothing to lose

But I had so very much to prove

And I had to get out of here

For the sake of myself and my family I had to move.

So I made a start and I headed right

I got on a boat to start my fight

The fight for my life, the fight for my rights

And I was filled with many fears and many delights.

In England I arrived

From my small island to the left

It was hard to talk

It was hard to catch my breath.

Then I met this wee English girl

With these long legs and an incredible smile

And I thought I might stay for a while

Just spend some more time with this girl and her lovely smile.

So I stayed for a while

With this girl and her smile

And I met her dad who was a good lad

And he gave me a job and I earned a few bob.

Time rolled by and by

And now if I left all this

This girl would certainly begin to cry.

So I now have to ask myself the question WHY?

Why should I stay and why am I trapped

I've been lead astray from the place I had mapped!

Things are not what they seem

And what ever happened to my very important American dream?

A Girl And A Boy

He was sitting on a sunny moat, alone and in a sombre state,

He was thinking of heading home as it soon started to get late.

And then this pretty young girl arrived and asked the boy

"Would you like to play with me?"

"No" said the boy " I'm not very happy today, not very happy, not very gay

And it's now becoming late, too late in the day."

"Don't be so silly" she said

"Come and play with me, we can be happy, we can be free."

"I cannot" said the boy. "For you have not tamed me, so we can't be happy and free."

"Well how do I tame you in order to be, so we can be happy, happy and free?"

Asked the girl tossing her hair that was full of curls,

She was wearing a pretty necklace that looked like pearls.

"You have to sit down a distance away,

Be by my side for a while then slowly slide,

Slide closer and closer telling me about yourself,

And so I can understand you and so we have nothing to hide" replied the boy.

"And when I have tamed you can we together play?

So I can make you happy, make you gay,

So we can be happy for all to see,

Together you and I, just you and me?" she asked.

"It's not so simple my petite Cherie,

For with taming me there with it comes a great responsibility.

If you desire my heart no matter how far apart or how far away,

You will always have this responsibility in order for us to play."

A perplexed look crossed over her pretty face,

A reaction granted not too out of place.

After some consideration the girl asked "Well can I see you again, any time soon?"

And it was becoming late and they noticed the rising of the moon.

"Yes when and what time?" asked the boy.

"What about tomorrow about the same time and maybe we could bring some toys" said the girl.

"Yes that would be just fine." he said

And the boy was filled with a feeling simply divine.

"Please don't be late" he said as she got up to leave.

"As I don't want to worry, I don't want to be deceived" exclaimed the boy.

"What do you mean? She asked

"Well I will be expecting you all day and if you are late a concern will burn in my heart,

I can feel it now as you are about to depart" said the boy.

"If you are late my heart will skip a beat,

I will be pacing all around upon my two feet,

My stomach will be sick and my eyes will weep,

If this responsibility you do not keep" He continued.

And with that the girl left.

The Mirror

Your personal animated expression

In an opposite reflection

That of yourself in your mirror

A mirror to see only your exterior

Does the mirror make you feel safe, inferior or superior?

You see yourself there

Do you stop and stare?

In the morning does the mirror give you a scare?

At night does it make you feel any more fair?

How long do you look and what do you see

From those windows of your soul that show your skin?

Is it with the mirror that you begin?

<u>We</u>

We walk, we run

We suffer, we have fun

We laugh, we cry

We live, we die

We say hello, we say goodbye

We sometimes do nothing and sometimes we try

We tell the truth and then we lie

We hold on, we let go

We go fast, we go slow

We learn but we don't know

We go up and we go below

We look forward, we look back

We will stroke, we will smack

We will achieve and we will lack

We look and we hear

We will go far but want to be near

We are brave but feel fear

We breathe in and then out

We trust and we doubt

What is this all about?

<u>Hard</u>

It's hard work loving you

You're always late

And this makes me very irate

You make a terrible date.

It's hard work loving you

And all the things you forget to do

When you moan at me and make a big issue

And I have to hand you a tissue.

It's hard work loving you

You and your scatterbrain

Your random distractions can drive me insane

Your wonderful self is sometimes hard to maintain.

It's hard work loving you

But I love you still

You are my biggest thrill

And when you're not here I do feel ill.

A Life's Sentence

We began with an innocent childhood romance
We grew up together hoping it would be forever
We had fun as we laughed and played and grew
I remember back then I really liked you

 Now we have had children together
And because of them we are bound forever
They have given us such pleasure, our creation, our treasure
Back then I still really liked you

Then money, a mortgage, bills and insurance
A commitment, a trust I have made with you for our future
With our bricks and mortar for when we mature
This is me and you, but I'm now starting not to like you

I have now spent the best part of my life with you
I have the utmost respect for you and a love which is true
We continue committed and close together like glue
But now I don't think I like you

We have travelled together around this earth
Exploring as one to rekindle some sort of rebirth
Still I love you and we have plenty left to do
And yet I just still do not like you

My dear I have seen what you have seen
You have been where I have been
Now we are aging and we have developed some virtue
But never the less I still no longer like you

I do not know exactly what happened between you and me
I suppose things just changed that I did not foresee
This world has changed for me and you
And I just no longer bloody well like you

Only Love

I want to go back to where I once belonged
But if the truth be told I have never belonged anywhere
Nowhere I can think of, no place for which I have cared.
I still want to go back and start again
But I don't know when I started, when I started anything.

Some of this world I have been around
And yet I feel I have been treading the same old ground
I thought I was looking for something
But nothing could be found.

I experienced many things, I almost died
I have laughed so much I have also cried
I have learnt many things, yet I know nothing
I've been looking for answers only to find different questions
Going around and around in different directions.

I like to keep things logical and simple
But I find it surreal and complex
Sometimes I need an index but I am left feeling perplexed
I want to be content but as with many things end up feeling vexed.

I have been brought up and taught to believe
In a God that I have never heard from or ever seen
I have been taught and told to be good according to God
But I see so many things in this world that are evil and mean.

I am now much older than my younger self and it is getting late
But some years ago I accepted an invitational date
Which led me to love
Now the only truth I know is this love was fate.

Destruction

They build it up just to break it down
They build a town to watch it fall down to the ground
They change the children's faces into a frown
Make them cry tears because of you clowns.

Build it faster, build it higher
Build some more, build another new skyscraper
Build until there is no more grass and no more trees
Keep building and put Mother Nature upon her knees.

Build your bomb, make your gun
I hope these men responsible are having their fun
Destroying this planet until all is said, all is done
What stories you have to tell your children and your mum.

Keep building when there is no need
Build it to compete and because you can
Build it for greed and glory
You silly fools I'm now bored of this story.

<u>One</u>

There's always one
Who wants to spoil the fun
There's always one
Who will block out your sun.
There's always one
That will play the fool
There's always one
That's determined you lose your cool.
There's always one
To put you down
There's always one
Who makes you stress and frown.
There's always one
To hold up the queue
There's always one
To make a mole hill into a big issue.
There's always one
Who gets in your way
There's always one
To make your head shake in dismay.
There's always one
So be prepared
There's always one
And this dilemma can't be repaired.

<u>Dreams</u>

Dreams of drumming beats

Over and over that constantly repeat, repeat,

And torture me from my head to my feet.

Dreams of killing a man

I did not know

I sliced him quick

And he died slow.

Dreams of places I have never been

Getting lost in between

These lands and streets that I have never seen.

Dreams of cats scratching out my eyes

Dogs biting through my thighs

Family and friends arguing all night

And children kicking, screaming, crying and fighting.

Dreams of terror

Dreams of fear

Why does my mind allow these things here.

Dreams of torture

And dreams of despair

Dreams of dying

And being trapped in a lion's lair

These dreams of mine are far from fair!

I Don't Like You

I don't like you
You give me a headache
You are a heartbreak
Now leave me alone for heavens sake.

I don't like you
You're a leech you're scum
You're as torturous as a screw thumb
With you I am surely done.

I don't like you
You fool, you pain in the arse
I knew you never had any class
To me you're as useful as broken glass.

I don't like you
You and your mentality
You and your vulgarity
And your consistent banality.

I don't like you
You bring me down
You wear the mask of a clown
And all you do is make me frown.

Eden

The devil on my left

And god on my right

Still the same struggle

And still the same fight.

Look but don't touch

Smell but don't taste

And all these juicy apples going to waste

Such ridiculous contradictions in this place!

He gives me a woman

And the lord takes a rib

Then he makes me wear a leaf of fig

Now things are different with consequences big.

Safe

An eye for an eye

A tooth for a tooth

This told to me during my youth

And in this there may be some truth.

A punch for a punch

Tit for tat

These sticks and stones

Could certainly break my bones.

So I choose to save my eyes

And save my teeth

And the ground I don't want to be underneath

And be presented with a wreath.

And so not to cause my family, friends and loved ones grief

And not to be surrounded by those already deceased

I'll turn the other cheek

And save myself some relief.

Panic

There's a panic in my heart
What with the dying art of conversation
Now a world apart with this technological civilisation
It makes me panic on occasion.

There's a panic in my eyes
When I hear or see the news
Of what's been destroyed or lost
And our greed to gain no matter the cost.

There's a panic in my mind
Due to things in this life, the terror, the strife,
The quiet man who butchered his children, then his wife.
These things I see and find, the inhumane and just the unkind.

There's a panic in my gut
As I can see the end is in sight
And after all this greed and sin
I can foresee the dying of the light.

What Is It?

It disappears in the dark, the mist, the cold and rain
And it does not care for your pleasure or pain.
It disappears in the sea and the sand
Which you held tightly gripped within your hand.

It disappears into the sky
Among moments flying by
And into the light it continues forward and resistant.
It is recalcitrant, fast and it does not last an instant.

It comes from the past
And have no doubt it will last
It will outlast you and all you ever do,
And sometimes it will make a fool of you.

It does not hide, confide, decide collide or abide.
It is a relentless mistress
To whom all and everything shall eventually be addressed
And even God shall be dismissed.

Ups And Downs

Fly into a sky of clouded questions

Dive into a sea to find a deep dark mystery

Concerning this land of man

A land we struggle to understand

We watch and wonder and ask ourselves

What was the original plan?

We reach for the zenith

And then suffer the fall

Once a smile so big

Now tears so small.

It will crumble no matter how tall

It was once remembered now you forget it all.

Broken

I saw her there below my window
This frail lady who resembled a shadow
She was randomly approaching the passing cars and men
Stopping them for money none of which found this funny

She was skinny as a rake this woman begging
Scratching and scraping and all alone
You could see her head and heart was aching
Just as this Sunday morning was breaking

Then she sat down upon a curb
She was muttering, confused, very disturbed
A can in hand she could barely stand
And I hope later she will find herself on better land

The Church Bells

I hear the church bells ringing

And I wonder if they sing or they cry.

Do the bells cry for loved one's dead

Or sing for the married with all their future still ahead?

The church bells I hear either singing or crying

Do they ring and chime for the living or the dying?

Echoing through the rain or the sun

Are they for an ending or for something that has just begun?

Do they sing for a bride dressed in white

Who is celebrating her moment of pure delight?

Or cry for the crowd in black who grieve a sudden heart attack?

The bells toll for the white and the black.

Life

Our time is running out

No matter how loud you scream

No matter how loud you shout

This is what life is all about.

Have no doubt one day you will die

But we do our best to defy

Defy this mortality

That makes us fear, that makes us cry.

Tick tock, tick tock

We are mice fighting against the clock

But soon enough we will be buried underneath a rock

And be trodden over by various flock.

Simply born to die

No need to ask why

This is the tragedy of life

The heart of our trouble

The source of our strife.

Life is a fuse lit with a spark

Life is a candle burning away in the dark

It melts away and leaves its mark

And then simply flies away just like a lark.

A Survivor

In one of my darker hours I was standing outside
And looking down at my feet
Suddenly I was lucky because what did I meet?
A beautiful flower growing out from a concrete street!

A survivor, a destined thing to make me see
To show me and to make me believe
That some things are not impossible
And that surly some things could be quite probable.

This flower grew on a polluted roadside
With nowhere to run and nowhere to hide
It was a delicate little flower violet vibrant bright
I could not believe it, but what a delight.

This flower in a road of poverty and shame
It had not wilted, it had in fact resisted, chosen to be uplifted
And it did not need any one else to blame
So I lifted my head and carried on now not feeling so ashamed.

The Dying Roses

The dying roses drop their petals to gather upon the floor
And this rose that is dying shall have them no more
So short lived and delicate as a feather
This tragedy will happen no matter the weather

The dying roses once so beautiful with colour
So attractive with scent
The pinks, peach, orange, red, yellow and white
They once stood tall, so vibrant and bright

The dying roses that stole the garden show
Blink and you'll miss them as they do not die slow
The pleasure they give is something not to last
And so very soon they are a thing of the past

__Hope Floats__

Hope floats upon a delicate zenith
Gliding above and around feather light
Expecting us to call
Whenever we hurt or fall.

Hope floats when all is lost
And all is gone
When we feel the pain
And nothing belongs.

Hope floats in our fragile hearts
When there are tears in our eyes
When we question God
And it's he we despise.

Hope floats like a small boat upon the sea
Facing the force of the sea's treachery
We hope to survive, we hope to strive
We hope in order to stay alive.

Do Go Gently

Do go gently into that good light
My only Nana with so much fight
Who we have cherished all our lives
Do go gently into that good light.

You were young and beautiful
In an ugly war torn time
But you lived, sang, and loved so bright
Do go gently into that good light.

A dedicated loving mother and wife
To which you devoted and gave your life
You were always there day and night
Do go gently into that good light.

And now you my precious Nana there above
Let it be known you were always considered, always loved
Now watch over us with all your might
And do go gently into that good light.

<u>The Departed</u>

Up and away into the peaceful night sky they go

Past the clouds that are willingly parting

For this loving couple

Who are now departing

A departing for these two who lived and moved together

For sixty years in tune

They now fly up hand in hand

Far and away beyond the moon

Now their souls reside above

United still and forever in love

The star crossed couple shine amongst the stars

Their spirits eternal and divine

Now always together beyond all time

Is There More?

Is there more to life than going faster?

I think at this rate it will end in disaster!

Is there more to life than going to war?

Killing each other and breaking God's law!

Is there more to life than killing this land?

Raping our fields and shifting our sands!

Is there more to life than a nine to five?

Living to work and struggling to survive!

Is there more to life than drink and drugs?

Going to pubs and clubs and behaving like thugs!

Is there more to life than buying things you don't need?

This shopping obsession and this need for greed!

Run

Run rabbit run
Dog chase your tail
Run you rats in your race
Anything to keep up the pace.

It's the faster you go
Do not be too slow
It's the need for speed
And the need for greed.

Run away, run away
Try to avoid the fray
Run, run to pay your way
Run, run to cease the day.

Faster

Lights change from red to green

And off their marks they go

To achieve speeds so dangerously obscene.

This is Moto GP and it's only for the lean and mean.

Their engines scream and roar

Their tyres shedding and melting

Upon an asphalt floor

And every second these men are knocking on death's door.

Born to go faster

This could all end in tragic disaster!

But the reason, the need for speed is beyond and far?

To be a racing superstar!

Apocalypse

Four horsemen descend

Furiously from a blazing sky

They and their horses coming to make amends

Flaming bright the end is nigh.

Hellish vibrations shake to the earth's core

Mountains crumble and fall to stand no more

Crumbling and crashing resorted to pebbles

They bury all us foolish rebels.

The sea she rises a mile high and with a huge roar

Flexing her mighty muscles to settle her score

She smashes and thrashes

So we exist no more.

We will burn, be buried, drowned, smashed, washed away

To cleanse all our abuse and our decay

This a result of the destructive mess we made

And this is how we get repaid.

Ding Dong

Ding dong and it's round one

And the fight for ones life has now begun.

The crowd is watching, waiting

Expecting and anticipating how you will fair

They can smell blood and fear in the air.

You take a punch

You give a punch

You feel the pleasure

You feel the pain

Bleeding and bruised

You fight to survive

You fight to see yourself stay alive.

You get knocked down

You try to get up

Get up before the bell

And sometimes it feels like you're going through hell

Ding dong, round two and there is the next bell.

The Politicians

To the so called politicians I see stalking around
Ambitiously cheating, lying, stealing, and making a killing
I would like to say I find you most profound
This excessive spending which you find so thrilling
I say to you I find it chilling!

Unashamed they are but they are to blame
They gather in the House of Commons, that hell of flames!
They sit there scraping together our taxpaying cash
Then rob it away and add it to their private stash.

Now I will not parade and shout this out loud
In order not to further anger the maddening crowd
So I write it down with pen and paper
And it makes me feel better to vent some anger.

I never wanted to be part of their systematic machine
A corrupt, undignified, political regime
It is far too ugly, far too obscene
And I can only hope that dirty politics will one day be clean.

Greed

You fat cats, you skinny rats

Smiling whilst driving two jags!

Smiling and scoffing

Stealing and dealing

I wonder if you have any feeling.

You bare faced liars

In whom we are supposed to trust

You twist and turn

For your needs must

And continue to defy all of us.

Conservative, liberal and pathetic labour

When will you do us all a favour

And stop your outrageous behaviour?

Where are our leaders

And where are the saviours?

The End

Rub and scrub it all out
Scratch and scrape it away
This is the time for the end
And have no doubt this is your final day

So pour it away
Leave it where you stayed
Bury it under the ground
And forget all you once found

The end is soon
So put away the moon
Pour away the sea
It's now too polluted for you and me

Pack up the sky
Turn off the sun
Put away the stars
And disregard Venus and Mars

There is no tomorrow
This time is a thing you only borrow
Now put away your sorrow
And fly off just like a swallow

I Miss You

I wake up in our bed and I reach out for you there

Next to me where you should be

Then I get up and go downstairs to make some tea

And I still make it for you and me

I go off to work and I hear you say

"Carry on darling I am ok

I'm just above you and always near

And I love you still, I love you dear"

I do my usual rounds about our place

And all I see is your beautiful perfect face

I want to tear out my eyes

As it's always you I could never replace

My dear I feel like I am dying without you

I'm cracking, snapping, and being crushed inside

I wanted to die by your side

And this look on my face I can't hide

Lonely the water is in this bath

Where I remember we touched and laughed

These bubbles are no longer fun

I just want to drown and be said and done

If only I could look into your eyes just once more

To feel your face, your hair, your skin, and such

There are no words to explain how I miss you so much

I just long for your magical touch

I miss you.

Index